Red on Tuesday

by Carolyn Townes-Richards

Living Through Literature

Aunt Curly's Collection - Illustrations by Diane Lucas

Trafford rev. 07/06/2023

 www.trafford.com
North America & international
toll-free: 844-688-6899 (USA & Canada)
fax: 812 355 4082

Carolyn Townes-Richards

Red on Tuesday

Special Thanks to
My Lord and Savior Jesus Christ

For
James Calvin Townes
AKA
"Red"

And
Phil Cleophas Townes and Theo Wood Townes
My parents

Two Snaps Up and 99 1/2 Kisses
To
Paul Richards Jr., My Loving Husband
Thanks for Reminding Me to Keep on Keeping On!

Todd Steele, My Brother-in-Law
Thank You for Devoting So Much Time to This Project, from Beginning to End.
Todd, You Are a Blessing to Our Family.

Annette Townes-Steele, My Sister Dearest
Thanks for Your Creative Ideas, and Also for Your Kids—Kristen, Jamie, Theo, and
Trinity.

Debora Townes, My Artist Sister
Thanks for Your Proofreading Expertise

Mia and Sonya
Thanks for Reading the Story and Confirming That
It Was Worth Telling It

Kim Williams-Anderson
Thank You for Typing This Story, for Recommending Trafford Publishing, and
for My Cute Hairdos.
Love you, Kim!

Tracy Montgomery
Thank You for Your Support

John and Beulah Moore,
My Barber-Scotia Family for Life

Dr. Alfred A. and Karen Bernard
Dr. Creflo and Taffy Dollar
Dr. Charles Stanley
David T. Demola and Family
Thank You for Impacting My Life with the Word of God

PROLOGUE

Red's story shows that small wrong decisions often lead to big mistakes. Each wrong decision that he made contributed to the beginning of a very sad series of events in his life. From his life, we see that the little, day-to-day choices we make are very important. They prepare us to make right choices when the "big" decisions come. The wisdom to make right choices in small and large matters is a gift from God.

Many aspects of Red's life are like familiar scenes in our society today. The words change but the essential message is the same. Red needed to renew his mind. He was stuck in an old paradigm. The strong holds of unforgivingness, anger, and lust gripped him. Red was not open to advice. For years, his mind was closed. He wouldn't listen to advice unless it reinforced the decisions he'd already made. Red continued to look for the path of least resistance. Very seldom did Red consider the consequences of his choices. To seek, hear, and heed the advice of good counselors would have been a much wiser choice for Red. Instead, he decided to lean on his own understanding and on the foolish advice of others, with devastating results.

Chapter 1

"Pinky" Joins Our Family

Everyone was so excited when he arrived. He was just fifteen minutes old and already lifting his head, looking around, staring into the eyes and smiling faces of his family. Grandma and Daddy just couldn't get over how that little rascal was carrying on. He was so alert on his debut on earth. They told everybody who visited Mama, "That boy's going to be something else. He's already looking around to see what he can get into. He's every bit of Theo." Theo was our mother.

Eager to see if Grandma was right, I moved closer to the bed to get a better look. I was amazed! How could it be? I was looking at my mama. Or at least it seemed as if I were. He looked just like Mama! He was a tiny little Mama. They kept saying "he," so I realized that the baby wasn't just like Mama, because Mama and I were girls.

I was a bewildered kid trying to figure out how this all had happened. Out of nowhere, I had another brother.

It seemed strange to folks that Mama had three kids and none of her children looked anything like her. It always annoyed her when people asked, "Are those your kids?" You'd never guess what her response was and I'd never fix my mouth to repeat what she said most of the time. That was probably the main reason there was so much controversy over this new member of our family.

I wasn't so happy about all of the attention being given to this new kid on the block. But of course I went along with all the hoopla. After all, he was really cute and surely looked like Mama. That was a good thing. She was a beautiful lady. A black woman with hazel eyes and red hair was a very cool thing to people in the South back in those days. Did I want to look like Mama? Yes, I did! Was I a little jealous of my new little brother who looked like her? Yes, I was! But I soon got over it. Better one of us to inherit her beauty than none of us.

My big sister nicknamed him "Pinky." Ridiculous, huh? She gave him that name because his skin was pink. "So, what will my nickname be?" I asked. "I gotta think of something," she said. She seemed a little irritated that I had asked. I walked away thinking, what is the matter with her? Was I wrong to ask that question? They were making such a fuss over Pinky that they forgot I was ever there.

Once I got used to the "green-eyed monster," things got better for my brother and me. I accepted the fact that Mama wasn't going to give him away, so I had to make the best of it. As we grew older, we became friends. We played cowboys and Indians, jump-rope, hopscotch…you name it, we played it. Believe me: I was very glad my mom didn't give him away. I loved him so!

Occasionally I would wonder aloud, "How did this guy get to be so lucky?" He was born on a Tuesday, July 4th. He was born in the summertime, when the living was easy. Schools were closed; family and friends were visiting, cooking out, and playing loud music; people were happy, dancing, and celebrating. It was a time of the year when we had good old-fashioned summer fun.

Pinky was the only one in our family born in July. Was that a problem? It was not a problem to most folk, but in my mind it couldn't get any worse than that. He'd be getting over like a fat rat. Just think about it: he was the baby boy; he looked just like Mama; and he had a birthday all to himself. Do you think that sounds silly? Well, it is not! I know that everybody born has a birthday; I'm not talking about that. I'm talking about unusual birthdays within one family.

My mom and dad did something that should have gone in the *Guinness Book of World Records*. Listen to this: There were three children in our family.

The first daughter, Chris, was born on September 3rd. Two years later, just minutes after September 3rd, my mother had a son named Phil. Two years later, my mother birthed a wonderful, blessed child named Carolyn. That's me! All three of us had to celebrate our birthdays on the same day. Sometimes there was only one big cake to be shared by all and one happy-birthday song for the three of us. How could a girl feel important, on a special day like that, with no preferential treatment directed toward her? Now you understand why I had a problem with this situation.

I grumbled and complained about it for years. Then, wisdom taught me that celebrating life with the people I loved was a most precious gift.

He had a birthday all to himself.

Chapter 2

Love, Trust, and Friendship

Elementary-school days were fun with my little brother, who was now a big boy. He was what people called a real boy. That meant he was adventurous, wild, and a risk-taker…all of the things my mama didn't like. She called it living too close to the edge. In other words, it was dangerous. Pinky frequently had to be told, "Stop that. Don't do that! Didn't you hear what I said, boy? You'd better listen!"

He was a real busybody. I enjoyed his energy. It was as though Pinky had an Ever-Ready battery inside, always ready to take a challenge. Mom's verbal and physical reminders meant nothing to him. He was like a wild-alley cat.

Mom gave me the job of watching him. I didn't like that job. I guess she delegated the job to me and not to our older siblings because I was with

Pinky most of the time. Any time he got hurt, somehow it was always my fault. I resented having that responsibility. Pinky was a difficult boy who thought he knew everything.

Cheating and antagonizing Pinky was my way of punishing him for getting us in trouble with Mom. I paid the price for that in the following years. I realized I would never lead or guide him if he didn't trust me. I had to work hard to regain his respect, trust, and friendship.

As we matured, we learned to talk about our daily school experiences. We'd identify the positive and negative situations that we confronted at school and then skirted off to tell Mama how we had handled it. We made some good and bad choices. But Mama was just thrilled that we were trying to solve problems on our own.

Chapter 3

Making Wise Choices

The thought of going to high school was most exciting for me and for James, aka Pinky. It was our first opportunity to establish new friendships outside of our immediate family and the church. Choosing friends was a big deal in our household. "You have to choose carefully," Mom said. Mama told us early in life that a man is judged by the company he keeps. For Mama, a person's character spoke volumes. Mom's favorite sayings were, "Be careful what you sow because that is what you'll reap," and also, "Be careful what you say because words create your world." She planted those seeds in us early, so that we would make wise choices. Some of us listened and obeyed, and some of us didn't.

I wasn't a lot like James. He and I were complete opposites when it came to choosing friends. Even though I sometimes "hit it off" with people, I would always take it slow. For me, friendships had to be established gradually in order to give both parties an opportunity to find out about one another's traits, interests, and values. James had the kind of personality that would allow him to meet people and they'd either hit it off or they'd want to hit him. He had a "red-hot" temper. He was fine as long as you didn't bother him.

James liked to hang with the older crowd. He said he had outgrown the juvenile friendships we had experienced when we were younger. His basis for friendship no longer focused on physical accessibility. You know how young children sometimes say, "She's nice," or "He's mean." His friendships now emphasized the need for psychological compatibility. He chose friends who spoke the same language and who shared similar interests and outlook on life.

I had a real concern about the outlook and interests of his older buddies. In my view, they were not role models that would inspire or encourage James to make choices that would influence his life positively. He needed to make choices that would help him become a productive citizen. It appeared that James was just happy being around them, listening to their stories and jokes as they drank beer after beer. I believe James felt acceptance from those older men as they talked about their life experiences.

I can remember this guy named Mr. Frankner that James used to hang out with. James laughed as he told me how Mr. Frankner drank a whole bottle of Thunderbird fortified wine as if it were water. "He was mad at his wife," James explained. "How did drinking a pint of Thunderbird help him with the situation with his wife?" I asked. "I guess he went to sleep and forgot about whatever problems they were having. I'm telling you now, Carolyn! Do not say a word to Mama about anything that I tell you. If you do, I'll never tell you anything that's going on in the streets." Reluctantly, I agreed to keep it a secret, but I never stopped telling him how I thought those people were not good for him. They didn't seem to be going anywhere in life. They were not even trying! They were just sitting around, drinking and talking about bad experiences. They didn't appear to be looking for a way out of their lifestyle.

It was clear that associating with older people wasn't the problem. There were many older people in our community who could have made a very positive influence on James's life. He had chosen the wrong older people. The ones he chose appeared to have lost their way in life. They were making bad choices and influencing the life of a young boy, as they traveled down their own path of no return. It was evident to me that these men and James had similar spirits.

James didn't realize that he had the power to observe their lives and listen to their stories, but not buy into that lifestyle as an appropriate one for him. As a big sister, I reminded him that there were good and bad choices. In the end, it was his choice. I could recommend what I thought was right, but everyone had (and has) the responsibility to choose for him or herself.

James always responded, "Don't worry, Sis, I've got a handle on things. Besides, I'm my own person."

Chapter 4

Sharing Our Gifts

I was in the eleventh grade when I auditioned for the cheerleaders' squad and James auditioned for the basketball team. It was on a Tuesday; I'll never forget it. For weeks, we'd talk about our plan of action. We agreed to practice diligently daily. James would echo my cheers and I would guard him as he dribbled down the court to make points. I was a good guard and I made him work hard to score points. He had mastered the skill of dribbling and was fast as lightning on the court. He knew how to work the crowd. People would gather around to watch him practice. They were amazed at this "pint-size" ball of fire who could hit three pointers every time.

Basketball was James's favorite sport and he was confident that he had the skills necessary to be an All Star player. So we both decided to do everything necessary to get ready for the big day. "I'll go to bed early, eat my vegetables, and pray," he said. I knew this was real important when he said he'd eat his vegetables. Mom had a difficult time getting us to eat anything green. So I was impressed with my brother's vow to eat his vegetables.

Chapter 5

That Horrible Tuesday

The auditions were closed to the public. Only the coaches and a few other school advisors were invited. We gave each other the high-five and off we went, bold and confident as ever.

I finished my audition before James and waited by the gym door to see his happy, blushing face when he walked out. "I don't have to ask how you did, 'cause I know you smoked them," I said. "So how did you do?" I asked, with a big smile. "Every time, that ball hit my hand slam-dunk," he replied. "You should have seen me, Sis! I jumped so high one time my head almost touched the hoop." I gleamed with joy for my brother. I was proud of this positive thing he was doing in his life. I loved him so!

On the following Tuesday, James returned for the final decision. When I saw him at the close of the school day, he wouldn't even look me in the eye. "James, what's wrong? Tell me, James, what happened?" I pleaded. He said nothing until he got home and Mama asked him the same questions. Then he responded, "Everyone said how good I did during the tryouts, so how come I didn't make the team? I can't believe they could be so unfair." He continued to say, "There were some guys who scored far less points than I did, and they made the team. Is it my height? Yeah! They're penalizing me because of my height. It just ain't right."

He was so disappointed. It had been a full rejection blow, which wounded his spirit. James was devastated!

Mom had observed his excellent performance on the court and agreed that he deserved to make the team. But she wasn't sure how to handle what obviously had turned into a real problem. She knew the danger of dreams deferred. Even though he was young and had his whole life ahead, as well as many opportunities to try again, she was concerned.

In an effort to ease his pain, Mom tried to make light of the situation: "Oh! Don't worry, sweetheart. Try again next year." She tried to ask questions about his performance, hoping that James would analyze how he had played that day.

That didn't work. "Maybe a visit with the coach would be helpful," she said to me. I told her that asking the coach to explain why they had chosen other students might cause more of a problem. "It may be viewed as poor sportsmanship," I reminded her. "He has no one to speak up on his behalf but me, so I have to at least inquire about this matter, which is so important to him," Mama said.

I could tell that Mama had made up her mind to make a visit to the coach. The thought of her making a visit to the coach concerned me deeply. Mama had a tendency to overreact to situations she felt had been improperly or unfairly handled. She had a reputation of being a no-nonsense kind of person. Her final decision, then, was to schedule a visit to the school to see the coach.

Mama visited Coach Dudley the following week. Mama's stern face and hazel eyes were always intimidating. She had an extremely serious look on her face that day. "Poor Mr. Dudley," I said to myself. I wouldn't want to be in his shoes.

Mr. Dudley was very cautious with his attitude and words as he explained the situation to her: "James is a very fine basketball player, Mrs. Townes, and I'm sure he is going to be on our team in the coming seasons. We were trying to give some of the senior-class students, who are also good players, an opportunity to play before they graduate from school. We are hoping that James will observe and grow as a team player. We would like for him to understand that he doesn't have to 'hog' the ball, but develop a team-player

grounded deep inside and turned to bitterness.... Going to school seemed to remind James of his disappointment. He appeared to be embarrassed. He would cut classes. Gym class was one that he missed weekly. He didn't want to see Coach Dudley's face. "James, you need to let it go," I pleaded. "You ought to listen to Mom. She's right: you can try out again next year. Remember, teachers talk. You don't want to get a bad reputation. They'll call you a sore loser."

"Yeah, if they call me anything other than James, I've got something for them."

"James, stop that! There's more to you than your basketball abilities! You know who you are inside. Names can't hurt you. You had better listen!"

Chapter 7

Mom's Cup Was Full

It was then that we began to realize how important a father's role was in the life of a family. James really needed a father. Our father had passed away at the end of our elementary-school years. He was quite young. As a matter of fact, he was only thirty-seven years old. Mom was only thirty-four when he died. By then, they had added two additional members to the family, Ann and Debbie. Just like my brother, they were cute as could be, but always in the way.

There were six children in the family now. I wanted to pin a sign on my forehead that read, "NO MORE CHILDREN, MOM, PLEASE!!!" I would add the word PLEASE hoping to deflect what might have been a physical-abuse case. I later realized I didn't have to worry about any more siblings, because my father was no longer alive and I doubted very much that Mom would ever remarry. You see, when you're a child, thirty-four seems very old. We thought that women of that age would never consider getting married.

Mom was a widow with the responsibility of rearing two boys. That was difficult for her. She was a real strict disciplinarian. That wasn't a bad thing. She just needed to balance the scales a little. She had to get an understanding that anything done to the extreme becomes an error. That included discipline.

Mom's feisty spirit was what she had been born with. Her method of discipline had been a learned behavior. What Mom did was simply pass down to our generation what she had experienced. Some parents do to their kids whatever has been done to them. You might call it generational hand-me-downs.

It became obvious that Mom's boys needed something that she couldn't give them: they needed a male spirit. It appeared that James really needed a father figure to help him discover that perfect power within him. He wanted to find the secret of his boyish soul. A male role model would have helped. That positive male model never showed up in his early-childhood life. So James rebelled against Mom relentlessly.

Unfortunately in those days, parents believed the old proverb, "Spare the rod; spoil the child." Sometimes I believe that was the only Scripture passage my mom knew. James felt the same way. However, that made it worse. To me, he was already hurting and longing for that something that Mom couldn't fulfill.

James felt helpless. So we began to pray, asking God to please give us that "spirit" we had heard about in church. We knew this would have done it for us. First and foremost, it would have saved us from Mom's disciplinary action…at least that's what we thought.

It was clear to us that Mom was hurting, too. She was brokenhearted; she longed for my dad. I would hear her crying in the night as she held the top hat he had been wearing when he fell to his death.

Maybe that was why she didn't come to church with us. She'd always make us go, but she'd never accompany us. I felt she was mad at God for letting my dad die so early in life, leaving her with six children, no job, a new house, and a car. These were wonderful things to be left with, but how would she pay for them? That was enough to make anybody mad and mean.

When I look back at our lives, I believe the principles taught in church would have helped her discover what was creating the pain, confusion, and disruption in her own life. Once she had discovered the truth, she would have gotten the strength and courage to stop it. The only way to get rid of a lie is through God's truth.

We suffered a long time due to a lack of knowledge. It wasn't until we were all adults that the truth set us free.

Chapter 8

A Fork in the Road

Graduating from high school was exciting. My college days had arrived! Somehow, I felt a little sad about leaving my family behind. I always felt that my being around had helped keep James in check. In spite of the years of teasing and taunting him, we had developed a bond of love and trust, which caused him to sometimes receive a word of advice from me.

Oftentimes I'd call home to talk to everyone. No matter what time I called, James was never there. Occasionally, my little sisters would tell me how strange he was acting. Mom expressed her concern about the friends he had chosen. Who could forget Mom's stance on one's choice of friends? Apparently James had, because the whole family was commenting on the peculiar actions displayed by his friends. It wasn't that Mom wanted us to stand in judgment of others, but make us aware of how right and wrong associations could affect our lives.

It became evident that James was making some real bad choices. From what they described, he had started "bending his elbow." That was a phrase that Southerners used when people began to drink alcohol. God knows that was a big mistake, indeed. The generation before ours had been proof enough for me—a monster I wanted no part of. I truly didn't want that for James.

Mom would question where he had been spending his time. She'd always ask, "What took you so long to come from school? Where is your homework? What happened in school today?" His answer was almost always, "Oh, nothing!" "That's strange," she'd rebut. "All day at school and nothing happened...!" Sure enough, when it came time to receive report cards, James had done "nothing." Sadly enough, he had missed so many days there was nothing for the teacher to do but give him a failing grade. I'm surprised my mom didn't make the headline news, "Mother Flew over the Coo Coo's Nest."

Our family spent time daily talking about the need to work together and be supportive of one another through good and bad times, so as to understand that all we had was each other and our Spiritual Father. Surely, that was what we needed most to travel along life's highway.

We held James's hand until he left Warrenton, North Carolina. That was the town we had been born and where we had lived until we graduated from high school. People called the area Red Hill. It was an area located just outside of Warrenton's urban district. Before they paved the streets, there had been nothing but red dirt.

Chapter 9

Getting to the Root of It

It was Tuesday, February 4th: Grandma's birthday. As we celebrated, James announced his desire to start a new life with new friends in the state of Georgia. This had been his decision and we were all happy for him.

Our older brother, Phil, had migrated to Atlanta, Georgia, after spending time in the army. James believed a new environment with his brother was what he needed to help him get back on track. What people often forget is that they "take themselves along" wherever they go. A change of physical location is often good; a change of mind and attitude, though, is of equal importance. That kind of change requires work. A person must have a real commitment to change. He or she must get rid of "stinking thinking." He or she can't continue to do the same things the same way and expect different results. Believe me, change is not change until there's tangible evidence of change.

For about ten years, James experienced what appeared to be the good life. Beautiful clothes, fine cars, and both pockets full of money. Every time he visited Mom, he was immaculately groomed, from the top of his head down to his little, seven-and-a-half-sized feet. "What a great job he must have," I'd say to myself. I then began to second-guess my decision to go to college. It looked like Georgia was the place to be.

Our brother Phil was an entrepreneur. James partnered with him for some years until he felt it was necessary to gain money at a faster pace than the job as a horticulturalist could provide. We were amazed at the progress he had made in such a short time in Georgia.

Soon it was like history repeating itself. James had new friends. He no longer hung out with Phil. For long periods of time, Phil didn't know where James was or what he was doing. That wasn't a good sign, but he was a grownup. Our approach to interfering in the life of an adult was a little different. We had to inquire about his source of income in a very diplomatic way. You didn't want to be told to "mind your business." Besides, in some instances, the less you knew, the better off you were.

Sure enough, it wasn't long before we got the phone call that James was in serious trouble with the law. Mom and I left that Tuesday morning en route to Georgia. All the way there, Mom continued spilling out old proverbs: "'What's done in the dark will eventually come to light.' All of his money has to be spent on getting him a lawyer. Ya see, 'Easy come, easy goes.'"

My poor mom! You could just feel the hurt and pain she was enduring. I kept reminding her, "Please, don't worry, Mom. He's going to be all right." "I don't need this," she refuted. "Why can't this boy just listen?"

Chapter 10

Growing Responsibilities

Several years passed and James was off and running. We all hoped that it would be another new beginning. "How many new beginnings do we get?" I would ask Mom. "Each time you repent, I mean, seriously repent, you have an opportunity to start all over again," she would reply.

James was now a father. Oh, how we enjoyed his two children! They were the most adorable little James Calvin's in the world. It was nothing for Mama to just pick up herself and drive ten hours to Georgia to see them for just one hour. Within that short visit, she'd buy them everything they asked for. Then, back on the road again. All the way home, she'd talk about those children. "They look just like my James," she said repeatedly. What she was saying was that, in fact, they looked just like her.

At last, things were going well. In addition to his lovely children, James had a successful landscaping business with his brother. Then, all of a sudden, James's life was yet again hit by a devastating blow. At the young age of twenty-three, the mother of his children suffered an aneurism. She died instantly. I wondered if my brother could take much more. In my spirit I prayed, "Lord, can't you take away this cup?" I had heard people use that expression in church. They were asking God to change the plan for their lives.

All I knew was that I didn't want my brother to go through any more pain. It seemed it had always been one thing after the other. It just kept on coming. I trusted that it was all in God's hand. He knew the purpose of James's life. I loved my brother so much it was hard not to want to help God out. I wanted to write another script for his life. I wanted him to have an easier road than the one he was having.

Can you see me with a new plan for his life, a plan that would be better than God's plan? Impossible, don't you think? God knows, I had a hard-enough time trying to get James to do the little things I thought would have made a difference in his life. So I repented for questioning God. Then, I prayed for time to heal the pain. As time passed, God answered my prayer.

Chapter 11

Giving Back

Difficult as it was, my brother pressed on. It seemed as though the James Calvin I had known no longer existed. He was now known by his Georgia friends as "Red." Again, he had acquired a nickname after his skin color. Thin, withdrawn, and downtrodden, Red drifted from day to day. He changed jobs month after month. He began to isolate himself from everyone from the past. Unfortunately, that included isolation from his seven lovely children that had been born during the course of the years. His children longed to receive the love and care of their father.

Soon Red received a phone call from New York. He never expected that he'd be offered a job as a Home Health Aide. Definitely not in New York! "Me? Someone is requesting me as a Home Health Aide? You've got to be joking!" he said. Mama needed someone to care for her while the family screened various health agencies. She was suffering from a disease called Alzheimer's.

Red knew that I was there to guide him, so he agreed to take on the challenge. Besides, this was an opportunity to get Red out of Georgia. "This is my chance to give Mama some of the love and care she gave me," he explained. So off he went to the Big Apple.

For about eight weeks, Red duly cared for Mama in New York. Everyone was amazed at the loving care he gave her. It was so unusual for a male to be willing to take on a job of this nature. The elderly neighbors loved and admired him for this.

Red had gotten into the routine of caring for Mama. Then he ran into some old friends from Red Hill, who had moved to New York years before. Yes, you guessed it: the same old "bending-the-elbow," spirited friends who now drew him right back into that familiar world he had been trying so hard to stay away from in Georgia.

It wasn't long before he was leaving Mama fully alone for long periods of time. Sometimes he would forget to feed her altogether. It was obvious that this wasn't working out for either Mama or Red. So he returned to Atlanta.

Years passed. We heard nothing of Red for a long, long time. No phone call to see if Mom was okay…nothing! I thought that perhaps his silence was embarrassment whenever he would think that he'd lost a job working for his mother.

Chapter 12

Time Doesn't Wait

It was Red's fiftieth birthday. I wanted to do something special for him; something that would surprise him. I knew that he loved clothes and jewelry, so I purchased a gold chain and cross. I waited several days to get a phone call acknowledging receipt of the gift, but he never called.

A month later, I went to my local post office to pick up my mail. There was a pickup slip in the mailbox. Red's birthday present had been returned to me marked Person Unknown. I was so disappointed. I had wanted so much to make that day a very special one for Red.

I took a trip to Georgia later that year. I hand-delivered Red's belated birthday gift. It hurt me so bad to look in his weak, sad eyes, but I felt good to see him smile with such appreciation for the gift. We talked briefly. I slipped some money in his hand and off we went to visit other family members.

As I traveled home from Georgia, I cried. What good was all my knowledge of Biblical principles if I couldn't apply them? I wanted to use them to help Red. What could I do? I truly believed that, when we had the opportunity to help anyone, we should do it. He needed someone to show him unconditional love. I realized that I couldn't love him in isolation. I had to be around him to show him love, no matter how imperfect, irritating, and frustrating it could be.

Chapter 13

The Soul, Mind, and Body

June 2004: Red was diagnosed with pneumonia and admitted to Memorial Hospital. He was there for days before anyone in the family knew of his illness. He remembered the phone number of his oldest daughter, so the hospital's social worker was finally able to make contact with the family. They were so happy to know that the man they had labeled "homeless" had a family.

There was no way I could conceive of Red being viewed as homeless. Not my brother! He was from a well-respected family, didn't they know this? I tried to convince myself that the thought of him looking like a homeless person was impossible. There was no way he could've looked that bad...or was there...?

All I could offer Red at that time was prayer. There was nothing better to offer him than that. He had refused all other recommendations. My family and I prayed without ceasing.

Chapter 14

Feeding the Mind

Approximately three weeks later, Red was released from the hospital. He had recovered from pneumonia and was on his way to rehabilitating his mind, body, and soul. Yes, Red began Bible studies with our sister Debora. That was good news for all. We all wondered how she had gotten him to attend. She responded quickly, "It wasn't an option. We would eat our dinner, talk, and off we'd go to our weekly study." We all smiled and our inner spirits leaped with joy. "What had taken him so long?" we asked. We all agreed: Better late than never! This had been real progress for Red!

Just think: Red was doing something good to strengthen his inner being. "Thank you, Father!" I shouted. I was so thankful for my sister's desire to take him with her every week. My brother was among family again. I didn't have to worry.

I felt great peace about Red. Like the rest of us, God had purposefully planned his life. I had to be still and rest in that truth. At the time, my problem was to try to live not by sight, sense, and circumstance, because keeping my eyes on the physical Red hurt so badly. What I was seeing with my eyes was bad; what I couldn't see was worse. I believed that whatever was eating away inside of Red had surfaced on the outside. It was necessary for us to feed him not only food for his body but also food for his soul.

Chapter 15

Recognizing Grace

Red was slowly getting his health back and anxious to return into the workforce. He returned to the city's downtown area to get "daily" work with companies that employed handy workers to do day-to-day jobs and then paid them in cash at the end of the day. That suited Red just fine.

It was better than just sitting around the house. He wanted to be able to support himself or at least contribute to the household.

But soon Red was missing! For several days, our sister Debora drove and drove around town, asking the local workers if they had seen him. Finally, one Tuesday after work, she spotted what appeared to be an elderly man sitting under a tree. It was Red, sitting there crying. When he saw our sister, he said, "I just prayed, 'Lord, please reveal to my sister where I am.' Thank God you showed up!" They both wept. Again, she recommended him professional help. "You can't do it alone, Red. It's bigger than you. It's a stronghold!"

She contacted counselors inside the hospital. They praised her for the gallant effort and concern for her brother. However, the counselors told her that, from their many years of experience, they had learned that most people who are in a state of denial have very little success in their program. "You can encourage him to come," they said, "but he must clearly understand that there is a problem which needs to be addressed. Until that happens, you'll be more than likely wasting your time."

Chapter 16

Hearing—Not Listening

From mid-September through the end of October, our family had little or no contact with Red except for the occasional food drop-off. That was as far as we went.

Then a phone call came from the hospital: Red had suffered a fall, which had damaged his spine. He was paralyzed from his neck down. There was no way I could handle seeing him in this condition, I thought to myself. What could I possibly do to let him know I was there for him without looking at him face to face?

After I came to grips with the situation, I decided to see Red. I prayed all the way to the hospital. As I walked closer to his room, for the first time in so long the memories of Mama holding him in her arms flooded my mind. I asked God for the strength to endure what I was about to see. How could this be happening to my friend, my first playmate…? I loved him so!

I couldn't believe how alert Red was. He was still trying to lift his head from the pillow, against the doctor's advice. I remembered the fuss, when he was born, Grandma and Daddy had made about Pinky's lifting his head and looking around. It was a part of history repeating itself.

We stayed around Red's bed as often as visiting hours would permit. It was so difficult to look at him in that condition. Yet, we had to; he needed family more than ever. Between our jobs and responsibilities, we provided time to share the "good news" with Red.

For several weeks, he was able to whisper and make his requests known. Then there was just silence. Red's children and family shared love with him for the last time. Red's time was up.

I couldn't believe that my cute, little red-headed brother, who had caused so much excitement in our home on that Tuesday, July 4th, was no longer here. In a way, I was glad that Mama's mental condition wouldn't allow her to understand what had happened. Knowing that he was gone would have equally taken her life away.

Chapter 17

Looking Back

As I sat on a pile of red dirt at Forest Lawn Memorial, the burial ground where Red was laid to rest, it took me a moment to pull myself together. That red dirt reminded me of home. It looked like the red dirt on Red Hill, the very nickname of the street where we had been raised.

I tried to make myself find something good out of this situation. I thought of Mama's statement about new beginnings: "Each time you repent—seriously repent—you have an opportunity to start all over." I then realized this was Red's new beginning—his chance to start all over! On that fateful day, he could have fallen and never regained consciousness, like our dad never did. But Red had received a period of grace.

I know that he had time to make peace with his Heavenly Father while lying on that hospital bed. That brought me some relief. The most important thing was Red's soul. I had to keep reassuring myself in order to get through on that sunny and horrible Tuesday. I had to erase the thought that, even though he was now a saved soul, his life had been all but a wasted life. Who was I to judge Red's life, after all? At that very moment, I thought I heard Mama's voice saying, "Judge not, lest you also be judged."

Chapter 18

Moving Forward

Red touched the life of many in some good and not-so-good ways. Nevertheless, if you had ever met Red, you'd have never forgotten him.

As I reminisced, I wondered about the significance of Tuesdays in Red's life. There was something about that day of the week…. I remembered the Tuesday when he had tried out for the basketball team. Red had moved to Georgia for the first time on a Tuesday, February 4th. He had attended Tuesday-night Bible studies. And, of course who could ever forget that Tuesday, July 4th, the day he had been born…?

Finally, Tuesday, January 13, 2004: My last day with Red on earth, one I'll certainly never forget. He had indeed completed his assignment. I had this strange feeling that it had been a test. God had allowed Red to pass through my life to test my faith, my love, and my response to that senseless tragedy.

I realized there and then that everything weighs on something; nothing is insignificant in a person's life. Those things that seem so small have true meaning and develop our character. Ever since that loss, I have valued each day, and every moment has become a revered time to demonstrate love and care for others.

It was no longer about Red; it was about those of us left behind. It was about his mother, children, grandchildren, sisters, brother, and friends. I'd never seen such grief and sadness in the eyes of my family. I could only remind them, "This, too, shall pass."

I mustered enough voice to say, "Thank you, Red, for helping me endure the test. You're forever a part of me."

Then we all held hands as we stood by **RED ON TUESDAY**.

James Calvin Townes
aka
"Red"

James Calvin Townes
aka
"Pinky"

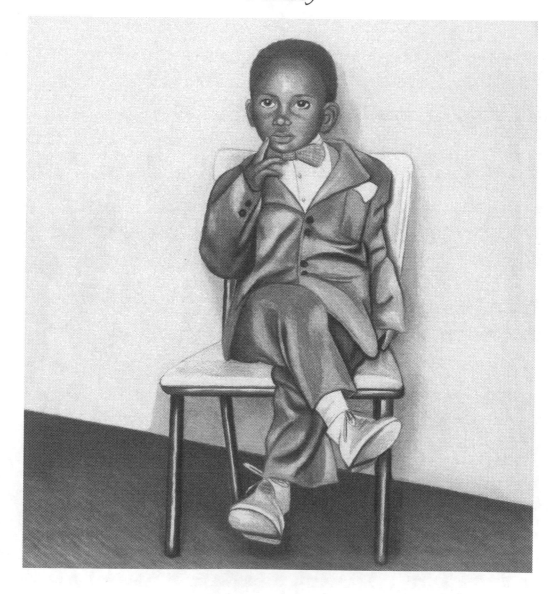

Questions
Literature Circle/Book Talk
Discussion

1. What was Red's real name at birth?

2. Where did he get the name "Red" and why?

3. What did Red's family notice about his character at an early age?

4. What was the very first problem that Red's sister had with him when he was born? Why was it such a problem for her?

5. What did his sister mean when she used the expression "green-eyed monster"?

6. Why did Red's sister believe it was necessary to build a trusting relationship with her brother?

7. Name one incident in which Red's mother was proud of something he had done with his sister when they were at elementary-school age.

8. Is establishing friends outside of the immediate family a positive thing? Explain why or why not. Identify evidence in the story that supports your position.

9. Why did Red's sister feel that friendship with older students was important? What do you think about friendships with younger and older peers?

10. In Chapter 3, Red was confronted with a problem that deeply affected him. Identify the problem. How did he respond to that problem? What would you have done differently? Was his mother helpful? Would a father have been more helpful? Explain.

11. Did the author state whether Red's sister ever got over the problem with the birthday situation?

12. Why do you think the author used the expression "Fork in the Road"? What does this expression mean to you? Describe when Red came to a "Fork in the Road."

13. What was at the root of Red's problem?

14 When did that problem begin to take root and to ground in Red's life?

15. What are some of the things that Red could have done to show his family that he was a responsible person?

16. What was the author's purpose for writing this story?

17. How did Red's family feed his mind?

18. Do hearing and listening mean the same thing?

19. What do you think about Chapter 15's title, "Moving Forward"?

20. Why do you think the author named the book *Red on Tuesday*?

Parenting skills
(With Loving Kindness Shall I Draw Thee!)

There are many wonderful things about large families. Unfortunately, there are also many trials and tribulations. Families with many children and where the parents get along poorly—where there is drug abuse, alcoholism, or where there is only one parent around—have their share of child-rearing problems. In such families, the parents may not have the physical or emotional energy it takes to reason with children and to be responsive to their needs. They may not have the energy it takes to set limits on their children's behavior and to enforce those limits. Thus, those children, from an early age, might defy their orders and fail to follow family rules.

Young children who haven't learned to comply with their parents' rules and requests are at risk for a variety of serious problems later on in life. These children, the majority of them boys, may be shunned by their peers, do poorly in school, and become either juvenile delinquents or adult lawbreakers, or both.

Oftentimes the trouble lies in the parents' inability to handle the "problem" child and a vicious circle is in effect, which causes things to go from bad to worse.

Sometimes parents with unsuccessful child-rearing styles can benefit from training in family-management skills. These parents need to learn how to react to their children's behavior in an appropriate and effective way—by giving positive attention when the child is being cooperative, and by promptly and firmly dealing with misbehavior before it has a chance to escalate.

(Eternal truths are most effectively learned in the loving environment of a God-fearing home. If you want your children to follow God, you must make God a part of their everyday lives.)

Red's offspring
(His Seeds Shall Be Great!)

James Calvin Townes, Jr.

Tabbatha Artelia Townes

Phil Jamison Townes

Brea Brock-Townes

Jeremy McKee-Townes

Jewell McKee-Townes

Fatimah McKee-Townes

Aunt Curly's Collections

Author Carolyn Townes-Richards

About the Author

Carolyn Townes-Richards is a native of Warrenton, North Carolina, and resides in New Jersey. She is a graduate of, respectively, the College of New Rochelle, Queens College, and Barber-Scotia College. Townes-Richards is an Assistant Principal at the Hempstead School District.

As an active member of the ASCAP Writers Association, Townes-Richards has published songs for Polygram Recording Company. She has received platinum-album status (1,000,000) for her vocal participation on the Tri-Star movie soundtrack titled *Breakin II Is Electric Boogaloo*.

Printed in the United States
by Baker & Taylor Publisher Services